D0510733

THE
MENTORING
POCKETBOOK

By Geof Alred, Bob Garvey & Richard Smith

Drawings by Phil Hailstone

"Mentoring is probably the most powerful developmental process people can experience. And when it works, it develops two for the price of one. *The Mentoring Pocketbook* is a no-nonsense primer for the first-time mentor or mentee."
Dr. David Clutterbuck, Co-founder, The European Mentoring Centre

"A most useful and informative book. I would commend it to anyone who is trying to develop their organisation using mentoring. A short read into this little book and you will undoubtedly do it better, and achieve better results."
Joan Rogers, Chief Executive, Hartlepool & East Durham NHS Trust

Published by:
Management Pocketbooks Ltd
14 East Street, Alresford, Hants SO24 9EE, U.K.
Tel: +44 (0)1962 735573   Fax: +44 (0)1962 733637
E-mail: pocketbks@aol.com
http://members.aol.com/pocketbks

This edition published in 1998. Reprinted 1999

© Geof Alred, Bob Garvey & Richard Smith 1998

ISBN 1 870471 56 3

British Library Cataloguing-in-Publication Data – A catalogue record for this book
is available from the British Library.

Printed in U.K. by: Alresford Press Ltd, Prospect Road, Alresford, Hants

CONTENTS

> "Mentoring is a process in which a more skilled or more experienced person, serving as a role model, teaches, sponsors, encourages, counsels and befriends a less skilled or less experienced person for the purpose of promoting the latter's professional and/or personal development. Mentoring functions are carried out within the context of an ongoing, supportive relationship between the mentor and mentee."

A mentoring researcher

HOW TO USE THIS POCKETBOOK

This book is a resource and support for those involved in mentoring at work.
It will be useful to anyone who is interested in professional and personal learning.
It is aimed mainly at mentors, but mentees will also find it helpful. It can be used in a
number of ways:

- **As an outline resource book:** it gives you a clear idea of how to prepare yourself
  for mentoring, conduct mentoring sessions, and maintain the mentoring relationship

- **For reflection:** it is a resource to consult, particularly when you are approaching
  a mentoring session or when you want to reflect, after a session, about what has
  gone on

- **To stimulate your development as a mentor:** the book provides a challenge and
  stimulus to reflect upon your role within your organisation, and what you value as
  a member of your organisation

Continued ...

HOW TO USE THIS POCKETBOOK

- **To stimulate your development as a mentee:** it may help you to develop your career and yourself personally

- **For discussion:** the book can be a focus for discussion with mentees in mentoring sessions and with other mentors in your network; it may also provide a focus for discussion with your line manager

- **To read selectively:** the book is designed to be read in any way which you feel appropriate, either the sections relevant to you or from cover to cover

Note Where this book talks of the 'mentee' others sometimes use the words 'protégé', 'mentoree' or 'learner'. 'Mentee' is our preferred term.

MENTORING IN ORGANISATIONS

MENTORING IN ORGANISATIONS

WHERE IT IS FOUND

Mentoring is rapidly becoming recognised worldwide as a highly effective human resource development process. Examples can be found in many diverse organisations from public to private sector, from service to manufacturing industries. There are mentoring programmes in:

- Manufacturing industries
- Financial services
- Tourism and leisure

- Petro-chemical industries
- Service industries
- Public sector

POSSIBLE USES

Mentoring is used in organisations for various purposes, eg:

- **Induction:** to help people become familiar with the organisation and get up to speed
- **Support for development:** to ensure effective learning for the future
- **Career progression:** to assist in identifying and supporting potential
- **Support for learning on the job:** to enhance job-related knowledge and skills for the present
- **Equal Opportunities programmes:** to ensure proper integration and fairness of treatment
- **Redundancy support:** to assist people in major transitions to new stages of their lives
- **Support in a new project or new job:** to ensure rapid assimilation and delivery
- **Within change programmes:** to help people understand what is involved in change

DEALING WITH CHANGE

Many organisations have gone through or are currently going through significant change. The pace of change is increasing. Generally, people in any organisation react positively to change when they take responsibility for their own development.

Organisations recognise this when they write their Mission or Strategic Statements. Good organisations also recognise the importance of the role they play in offering assistance to people during periods of change. Mentoring is one way in which organisations can provide this assistance.

MISSION STATEMENTS

The idea that people make the difference is often present in Mission and Strategic Statements. For example:

"Able and Co. will be a fast moving, customer-focused organisation, ensuring value for money, and getting results through well-motivated staff."

"We recognise the importance of our human assets in delivering our company's mission."

"Jones Ltd's people will be empowered to secure effective and exceptionally responsive service to customers."

"We aim for extraordinary customer satisfaction through a people-focused strategy."

"Our mission will be achieved through the willing efforts of all our people."

"People are the fundamental asset on which the company's success will be based."

MENTORING IN ORGANISATIONS

VALUE STATEMENTS

Many organisations establish a set of values in order to describe how their business should operate.

Values are often written down as part of the organisation's strategy, eg:

- To **delight the customer**, by providing the right advice, right information at the right time
- To **respect and value people's opinions**, through our equal opportunities policy
- To **focus on people**, by supporting and developing staff
- To **encourage openness in all our business dealings**, through developing a 'blame-free' environment
- To **strive for excellence** in the delivery of all our services
- To deal with all our staff and clients with **fairness and honesty**
- To be viewed as a **'good' employer**

MENTORING IN ORGANISATIONS

VALUES

✔ **Mentoring** helps people to understand how a company's values are realised in the organisation. It helps them feel that they are making a worthwhile contribution.

✔ **Mentoring** has strategic development implications. It is consistent with the Investors in People standard and is often supported by the organisation's development and training strategy.

✔ **Mentoring** can make a contribution to the delivery of the Mission and Strategy and the achievement of objectives. It helps to uphold organisational values.

✔ **Mentoring** helps individuals to develop within the organisational framework.

MENTORING IN ORGANISATIONS

FROM THE FRONT LINE

> *"Mentoring helps people understand and work through change and so contributes to the achievement of the Mission or Strategy. Mentoring helps people to learn and supports self-development."*
>
> An experienced mentor

THINKING ABOUT MENTORING

THINKING ABOUT MENTORING

WHAT IS MENTORING?

In mentoring, the relationship between mentor and mentee is all-important.

- There is a high degree of trust and mutual regard
- The mentor helps another person become what that person aspires to be
- The mentor helps the mentee to realise his or her potential

SUPERVISOR

WHAT IS MENTORING?

You have probably been mentored already!
Many people can remember being helped by
someone who took an interest in their welfare,
shared their experience and knowledge with them,
and enabled them to develop.

Often they remember these relationships
as playing a crucial part in their personal
and professional development.

WHAT IS MENTORING?

A good mentor remembered:

"When I joined the organisation I was asked after a few weeks to find someone to be my mentor. I asked Peter since we worked in the same section and he was friendly and approachable. We set aside an hour a week so I could talk through issues that were concerning me. We ranged over a lot of issues, personal as well as professional. Peter would make sure we finished the meeting with action points that I would try to follow up on, and that would often be where we started from the next week. But I could always ask him questions between our meetings as well. It was valuable to be able to turn to him over the kind of small matters that you would hesitate to bother some people with, especially your line manager. Peter helped me to get a picture of the whole organisation and my place in it. Thanks to him I settled in quickly and built up a sense of how my career might develop and what I needed to learn in order to make progress."

IDENTIFY YOUR OWN MENTORS

Ask yourself the following questions:

- Who took an interest in my welfare and development at a time when I was taking on challenges, such as starting a new job?
- Who has been a useful role model in my life?
- Who helped me to uncover and use a hidden talent or ability?
- Who helped me face and resolve a difficult situation in my personal and/or professional life?
- Who challenged me to acquire a new vision and take a new direction?

These people have been your mentors.

FAMOUS MENTORS

There have been many well-known examples of the mentoring relationship throughout history, including:

- Haydn and Mozart

- Annie Sullivan and Helen Keller

- Bill Shankly and Kevin Keegan

- Peter Thompson and Tony Blair

- Brian Close and Ian Botham

MENTOR & MANAGER

As a **manager** you are concerned with the objectives of both team and organisation.

As a **mentor** you help your mentee to learn within the context of a supportive relationship.

Mentoring and managing are not completely distinct. Managers may often use mentoring as part of their line role. They also recognise the value of an employee having a separate mentor, as this will enhance the overall performance of the employee and his or her contribution to the team.

MENTOR & MANAGER

When the mentor is somebody different from the manager this does not have to be a threat to the manager's authority. The benefits of mentoring to the manager and his or her team will emerge in the form of greater commitment, motivation and learning on the part of the mentee.

It is important that:

- There is as much openness and honesty as possible between the line manager, mentor and mentee
- The confidentiality of the mentoring relationship is respected

MENTOR & MANAGER

"*One of the things mentors and mentees should do is to make sure that the mentee's line manager knows that mentoring is going on.*"

An experienced service industry mentee

THINKING ABOUT MENTORING

TYPES OF RELATIONSHIP

Mentoring relationships vary depending on the people and the character of the organisation concerned. They may be:

- **Open**   - able to discuss any topic
- **Closed**   - restricted discussion topics
- **Public**   - others know that the relationship exists
- **Private** - few know that the relationship exists
- **Formal**   - agreed appointments, venues and timing
- **Informal** - casual or a 'pop in anytime' basis

TYPES OF MENTEE

There is no blueprint for the ideal mentoring relationship. You may be a mentor to:

- A peer
- A team member
- Someone you know well, or
- Someone you have not met before

What is common to all cases of mentoring is that the mentee comes to view things in a new way. The mentor promotes change in the mentee, helping that person towards a new vision of what is possible.

MENTORING: THE BENEFITS

- **Mentee** - benefits by developing confidence, learning more effectively and quickly, and acquiring new perspectives
- **Mentor** - benefits by acquiring improved ways of working with people and satisfying the desire to help others
- **Both** - mentor and mentee benefit by developing a wider perspective on their organisation and work
- **Line manager** - benefits by having a more motivated and effective team member
- **Organisation** - benefits by having more fulfilled, committed, resourceful and motivated employees

MENTORING, COACHING & TRAINING

There is no simple distinction between these activities. However:

- **Coaching** tends to have a specific and tightly-focused goal (eg: helping someone to prepare for an interview board or to make a presentation to a client)
- **Training** tends to be wholly work-related and concentrates exclusively on someone's professional skills and concerns
- **Mentoring** goes further in offering support and advice to someone as a person, and may touch on any aspect of their life; the mentor may offer coaching or training from time to time as appropriate, but may also encourage the mentee to seek help from specialists in these roles

MENTORING, COACHING & TRAINING

In the United States and Canada there is a tendency for people to mean by 'mentoring' what Europeans mean by 'coaching'.

> *"I found the literature on mentoring confusing until I realised the term meant something rather different for Americans. For them it's much more a matter of bringing people on in their professional roles as quickly as possible, even of offering opportunities for high-flyers to race up the career ladder."*
>
> A personnel manager in manufacturing industry

MENTORING & APPRAISAL

Mentoring and appraisal use many of the same techniques. The difference between them is that:

Appraisal is part of a formal system which identifies strengths and weaknesses, and may be linked to performance-related pay, to opportunities for promotion or the requirement to undertake training.

Mentoring is not formally connected with structures of extrinsic reward - or penalty! The mentor is non-judgemental, and does not impose his/her views on any third party. The mentee can be candid with the mentor in a way that would be unlikely in the context of appraisal.

NOTES

THE MENTORING PROCESS

THE MENTORING PROCESS

GETTING STARTED

Although mentoring is a common, often unrecognised, activity, it is a form of helping that most people could develop further. Effective mentoring requires certain personal qualities and skills.

How will you know that you are ready to be a mentor? This is an important question. You can address it in a number of ways:

- Recognise and reflect on the mentoring you do already

- Talk to other mentors

- Talk to people you have already mentored (officially or unofficially)

- Consider the differences between mentoring and management

- Consider the differences between mentoring and other ways of helping, eg: counselling, coaching, appraisal

- Reflect upon your own experience of being a mentee

THE MENTORING PROCESS

GETTING STARTED

How will you know that you are ready to be a mentor?
You can also address this question by comparing your
attributes with those of effective mentors:

- Relevant job-related experience and skills
- Well-developed interpersonal skills
- An ability to relate well with people who want to learn
- A desire to help and develop mentees
- An open mind, a flexible attitude, and a recognition of their own need for support
- Time and willingness to develop relationships with mentees

Do you have these attributes? If so, you are ready to mentor.

GETTING STARTED

> *"I'm now about to become a mentor myself, having attended a mentoring workshop. I don't know if anyone I mentor will be fortunate enough to get as much out of the experience of being mentored as I did. But if I can contribute to someone else's development in some way then, hopefully, the experience will be rewarding both for the mentee and for myself."*
>
> A manager approaching the mentoring role

AREAS OF DEVELOPMENT

A mentor can help a mentee to:

- Understand appropriate behaviour in social situations
- Understand the workings of the organisation
- Acquire an open flexible attitude to learning
- Understand different and conflicting ideas
- Be aware of organisational politics
- Overcome setbacks and obstacles
- Acquire technical expertise
- Gain knowledge and skills
- Develop personally
- Adjust to change
- Develop values

THE MENTORING PROCESS

3-STAGE MODEL

Mentoring includes a number of processes. Different mentors have different strengths and work in different ways. Whatever approach or style you use, you need to work within a framework, to be of most help to the mentee.

A useful framework is a 3-stage model* of helping:

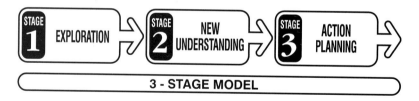

* Adapted from the 'skilled helper model' appearing in Gerard Egan's *The skilled helper: a problem-management approach to helping*, published in 1994 by Brooks/Cole, Pacific Grove, California.

THE MENTORING PROCESS

3-STAGE MODEL

The model can be used in a number of ways:

- To **reflect** upon what mentoring involves, and to **assess** yourself as a mentor
- As a **schedule** for a mentoring meeting - to work through the stages
- As a **map** of the mentoring process - to see what ground has been covered and what needs further attention
- To **review** the mentoring relationship over time, as the mentee moves towards achieving the goals identified earlier in the relationship
- To **enhance** shared understanding of the mentoring process and relationship, and to develop the mentee's ability to use the model independently

3-STAGE MODEL

> "Mentoring gives me a real buzz and makes me feel unbelievably good that somebody can learn and develop with my help. It has enabled my influence to spread in the organisation and thus assist the change process in a way which is more powerful than any other process I know."
>
> An NHS manager and mentor

THE MENTORING PROCESS

STAGE 1: EXPLORATION

Strategies

As mentor, you:

- Take the lead
- Pay attention to the relationship and develop it
- Clarify the aims and objectives of the mentoring
- Support and counsel

Methods

As mentor, you:

- Listen
- Ask open questions
- Negotiate an agenda

3 - STAGE MODEL

THE MENTORING PROCESS

STAGE 1: EXPLORATION
GETTING MAXIMUM BENEFIT

- Take the lead in creating a **rapport** with your mentee and an atmosphere that encourages exploration; show your **commitment** to the mentee, the mentoring process and the mentoring relationship

- Give it time, **be patient**; action plans come unstuck when rushed, and insufficient exploration leads to faulty understanding in Stage 2 and hence to inappropriate plans (investment of time and care in Stage 1 pays dividends later in the meeting and later in the relationship)

- Help your mentee to arrive at his or her own answers

- Resist the temptation to give advice or tell the mentee what to do (there are occasions when advice and direction are helpful, but not in Stage 1)

THE MENTORING PROCESS

STAGE 1: EXPLORATION
POSSIBLE QUESTIONS/COMMENTS

As a mentor, you might say:

'What would you like to talk about today?'

'Let's explore this issue some more.'

'What I understand you to be saying is... (paraphrase/summarise). Does that seem right?'

'Shall we start by recapping on our last meeting?'

'Tell me about your experience of...'

'You've said very little about X, but that seems to be central to the issue we are discussing.'

THE MENTORING PROCESS

STAGE 1: EXPLORATION
HOW LONG DOES STAGE 1 LAST?

This is an important question but it does not have a straightforward answer. It is important to think about how much time to give to exploring an issue so that you can assess progress.

Much depends upon the topic being explored:

- If it is something **significant**, related to changes in personal or professional attitudes and behaviours, you may find that you need to explore an issue on and off for several months or longer

- If it is a **practical** topic, related to knowledge or skills, it may take a few minutes or a few hours

Either as mentor or mentee, if you feel that you are stuck in a rut of endless exploration with no progress, it is time to talk about your relationship.

THE MENTORING PROCESS

STAGE 2: NEW UNDERSTANDING

Strategies
As mentor, you:
- Support and counsel
- Give constructive feedback
- Coach and demonstrate skills

Methods
As mentor, you:
- Listen and challenge
- Ask open and closed questions
- Recognise strengths and weaknesses
- Establish priorities
- Identify developmental needs
- Give information and advice
- Share experiences and tell stories

STAGE 1 EXPLORATION

STAGE 2 NEW UNDERSTANDING

STAGE 3 ACTION PLANNING

3 - STAGE MODEL

THE MENTORING PROCESS

STAGE 2: NEW UNDERSTANDING
GETTING MAXIMUM BENEFIT

Stage 2 is the **turning point** in the process. New understanding is experienced in a number of ways, depending on the individual and the importance of the issue in hand. Be flexible and resourceful, ready to move forward (and sometimes backwards) empathically and constructively with the mentee.

New understanding often releases energy, it can be exciting. Once your mentee begins to see things differently, offer **encouragement**. Progress can be rapid but again - **don't rush**.

Arriving at a new understanding can be uncomfortable: the mentee may be resistant. Then progress can be slow and erratic. This could signal the need for more exploration.

Be ready to return to Stage 1, eg: 'Now that you appreciate better the impact of working with new colleagues, perhaps you would like to look again at your thoughts about further training'.

THE MENTORING PROCESS

STAGE 2: NEW UNDERSTANDING

GETTING MAXIMUM BENEFIT (Cont'd)

If the mentee is resistant, be **supportive** and **sensitive** so that when you **challenge**, your mentee is receptive and able to learn.

Challenge **positively**, eg: refer to the mentee's achievements, positive qualities and potential, as well as offer constructive criticism of current behaviour, perceptions and attitudes that may be causing problems. **Be patient.**

New learning can make the mentee feel vulnerable, especially if it requires recognition that old ways of behaving have outlived their usefulness and there is a need to change.

THE MENTORING PROCESS

STAGE 2: NEW UNDERSTANDING
GETTING MAXIMUM BENEFIT (Cont'd)

Help your mentee **consolidate** his/her learning, to hold on to the fruits of the exploration in Stage 1. One way to do this is to **share stories** and **experiences** of your own.

Don't share too soon, as new learning can be fragile at first. There is a risk of taking the mentee away from his/her own agenda.

Reflect back and clarify what the mentee has learned and the implications of **new developmental needs, goals and aspirations**.

STAGE 2: NEW UNDERSTANDING
POSSIBLE QUESTIONS/COMMENTS

As mentor, you might say:

'The way you're talking now reminds me of the time I...'

'What is there to learn here, what's the most important thing to work on, now that you're seeing the situation differently?'

'Well done, that feels like a breakthrough.'

'Now that doing X looks like a viable option, there is some useful information I could share with you.'

'You've shown real commitment in the situation, but there are also things you've done that you regret. Is that a fair comment?'

THE MENTORING PROCESS

STAGE 2: NEW UNDERSTANDING
HOW LONG DOES STAGE 2 LAST?

Reaching new understandings is key to the next stage. Action born out of poor understanding is always flawed! This stage should not be rushed, although reaching a new understanding can happen quite spontaneously during a Stage 1 discussion.

It may take hours, days, weeks, months and even years to fully understand a complex issue.

The timescale is dependent on experience, the nature and complexity of the issue and the quality of the conversations in the mentoring discussions.

THE MENTORING PROCESS

STAGE 3: ACTION PLANNING

Strategies

As mentor, you:

- Examine options for action and their consequences
- Attend to the mentoring process and the relationship
- Negotiate an action plan

Methods

As mentor, you:

- Encourage new and creative ways of thinking
- Help to make decisions and solve problems
- Agree action plans
- Monitor progress and evaluate outcomes

STAGE 1 EXPLORATION → STAGE 2 NEW UNDERSTANDING → STAGE 3 ACTION PLANNING

3 - STAGE MODEL

THE MENTORING PROCESS

STAGE 3: ACTION PLANNING
GETTING MAXIMUM BENEFIT

When Stages 1 and 2 are done thoroughly, Stage 3 is usually straightforward and uses familiar **people management/development skills**.

Plans are followed through when the mentee **owns** the solution. Give advice and direction sparingly. Enhance **commitment** to change by clear agreements and target setting.

Look after the **relationship**, discuss its progress with your mentee. **Don't expect every meeting to end in an action plan.** Sometimes the action will be to meet again, and that will be progress enough. Affirm and celebrate progress.

STAGE 3: ACTION PLANNING

POSSIBLE QUESTIONS/COMMENTS

As mentor, you might say:

'Let's look at the pros and cons of this option.'

'Let's spend some time talking about the mentoring itself, as we agreed to review after three months. Perhaps we could do it over lunch.'

'How can I help you do this? Perhaps a demonstration of X would help.'

'Now that you've decided to do Y, is there anything you need to do first?'

45

STAGE 3: ACTION PLANNING
HOW LONG DOES STAGE 3 LAST?

The important point here is that it can be very tempting to rush to action. This is often true when there is a lot of pressure on people to perform at work.

The quality of action is firmly linked to the quality of Stages 1 and 2.

Sometimes the action phase is immediate but, in the case of complex attitudinal and behavioural issues, it may take weeks, months or even years to fully develop.

Mentoring is seldom about 'quick fixes'. If it is to work really well, a longer-term view is necessary.

FROM THE FRONT LINE

> *"To be a successful mentor enjoy what you're doing as well as BELIEVE in your mentee. Do not hesitate to ask for help from another mentor with special expertise. Friendship and rapport are important. The rewards of being a mentor are similar to the enriching experiences of meeting interesting people and facing the challenges of solving difficult problems. A good mentor, therefore, brings enjoyment of people and ideas and a strong belief to the mentoring situation."*
>
> A mentor with many years' experience

FACILITATING LEARNING

Another way to look at mentoring is by making use of the learning cycle, based on Kolb's theory of experiential learning. An awareness of the cycle can help the mentor and mentee to focus on the mentee's learning.

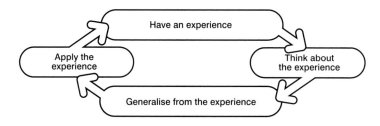

THE LEARNING CYCLE

The mentor helps the mentee round the learning cycle by asking questions such as:

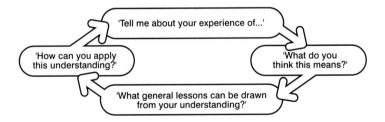

'Tell me about your experience of...'

'What do you think this means?'

'What general lessons can be drawn from your understanding?'

'How can you apply this understanding?'

FINDING A MENTEE

In your organisation, your mentee may be somebody you know already.
An existing relationship may develop into mentoring.

Your organisation may have a formal mentoring
scheme or some system for facilitating
mentoring. Then a match will be arranged.

It may be policy in your organisation for
employees to be assigned a mentor in certain
situations, for instance as part of induction for
new employees or when an employee
takes on new responsibilities.

THE MENTORING PROCESS

WHEN MENTEE CHOOSES MENTOR

Mentoring is primarily for the mentee, **for their welfare, development, progress,** within the context of their responsibilities and ambitions within the organisation. A person seeks a mentor because s/he recognises the need for mentoring support, or the need is recognised by a concerned third party (eg: the person's manager).

As a mentor, what do you think would be helpful for your mentee to know about you? Put yourself in their position. The information you give about yourself needs careful thought. It can help to write it down or talk it through with a trusted friend, or your own mentor.

'could I have your thoughts on . . . . .'

BEING A MENTOR

Keep in mind that a mentee will benefit from your:

- Knowledge
- Experience
- Personal qualities and skills

BEING A MENTOR

KNOWLEDGE

Think about your knowledge of the **organisation:**

- Its politics
- Its culture
- Its history
- Its character

THE MENTORING PROCESS

BEING A MENTOR
EXPERIENCE

As a mentor you will draw on your experience of:

- Facing difficulties
- Meeting new challenges
- Being helped, being a mentee
- Working with others, contributing to an organisation
- Achievement, success, failure
- A variety of organisations/working practices
- Being responsible for yourself, your actions and reactions to others and situations
- Trauma and setback
- Coping with stress

THE MENTORING PROCESS

BEING A MENTOR
PERSONAL QUALITIES

As a mentor you will draw on your ability to be:

- **Enthusiastic** - genuinely interested in the mentee and his/her concerns, needs, dreams and aspirations
- **Motivating and encouraging** - to channel the mentee's energy into constructive change, new challenges and overcoming difficulties
- **Open** - prepared to share your own experience of similar issues, be honest about yourself, be honest about the mentee
- **Empathic** - able to appreciate how the mentee thinks and feels and behaves
- **Positive in your outlook** - able to appreciate the mentee's point of view and see solutions
- **A good listener** - able to really focus on what the mentee is saying without your own thoughts crowding out the mentee's words

FROM THE FRONT LINE

> *"Fit and chemistry must be considered when pairing the mentor and the protégé. If the two don't get along, it matters little what each can offer the other in terms of knowledge and skills."*
>
> Michael Zey, *Building a successful formal mentor programme*

THE MENTORING PROCESS

BEING A MENTEE

People learn how to be a mentee through being part of a mentoring relationship. With commitment, experience and practice, mentees become better at making the most of the mentoring process. Successful mentees:

✔ Accept **challenge** willingly; they are **committed** to the mentoring process

✔ Have **trust** and **confidence** in their mentor; they are willing to discuss issues openly

✔ Recognise that learning can involve taking **risks** in order to make progress

BEING A MENTEE

Successful mentees also:

✔ Want to be **active** in their development and see learning as a **continuing process**

✔ Make **progress**, and **recognise** when the relationship is reaching its natural end

When the mentee **owns** the process, the quality of learning is improved.

THE MENTORING PROCESS

MENTEES' EXPECTATIONS

Mentees who understand the value of mentoring and are committed to a mentoring relationship, expect to gain in some of the following ways:

- Be challenged
- Enjoy friendship
- Learn from example
- Learn from mistakes
- Receive wise counsel
- Listen and be listened to
- Become more self-aware

- Be coached
- Be supported and encouraged
- Learn how the organisation works
- Foster the mentoring relationship
- Share critical knowledge
- Develop greater self-confidence
- Be assisted in developing their careers

THE MENTORING PROCESS

MENTEES' EXPECTATIONS

New and inexperienced mentees may expect to:

- Be managed
- Be given answers to problems
- Be told what to do
- Have an easy ride
- Receive favours
- End the relationship when the immediate problem or issue appears to be sorted out
- Gossip
- Whinge

An inexperienced mentee may need a lot of support and gentle challenge.

FROM THE FRONT LINE

> *"Mentoring is about learning, and one thing I learned is how to be a mentee. In a way, this is the greatest benefit of all. Now it's as if I can mentor myself, and this includes seeking help when I need it. I'm also beginning to think I would like to mentor someone else."*

A mentee

WHAT MENTEES NEED

A systematic approach, such as the 3-Stage Model, increases the effectiveness of mentoring. At the same time, mentees look for different things, such as:

- A sounding-board
- A giver of encouragement
- A critical friend
- A source of emotional support
- A confidant
- A source of knowledge

THE MENTORING PROCESS

AREAS FOR DISCUSSION

Mentees and mentors talk about:

- The mentee's work-related issues
- The mentor's work-related issues
- Career development
- Time management
- Personal issues
- Domestic issues

NOTES

WORKING TOGETHER

THE FIRST MEETING

> *"I was assigned a mentor when I took up a new post and I very quickly realised how helpful he would be to me. He was approachable, enthusiastic and very capable, and I did not feel silly asking basic questions."*
>
> An inexperienced mentee

THE FIRST MEETING

KEY ISSUES

Preparation. It is helpful to have an agenda for each meeting. Reflect on the nature of mentoring, the process as well as the outcomes. Think about your commitment to using mentoring well and giving it adequate time.

Getting to know each other. Give this enough time; it is the basis of trust and working well together. Share experiences from your pasts.

Time. Your relationship will change over time. Many mentees and mentors notice that discussion topics widen and deepen.

Difficulties. Sometimes things may go wrong. Nothing can replace honest and open discussion about the relationship. Try to let others know about the existence of your mentoring relationship to avoid any misunderstanding or resentment. Keep the relationship under review.

Ground rules. Establish ground rules. These will include:
- **Confidentiality:** this is essential. Agree between yourselves the boundaries of the relationship
- **Time commitment:** how much and how often?
- **Location:** where are you going to meet?
- **Recording meetings:** will you record your meeting and, if so, how (a diary or log)?

MAINTAINING THE PARTNERSHIP

Like any worthwhile relationship, mentoring relationships have natural life cycles:

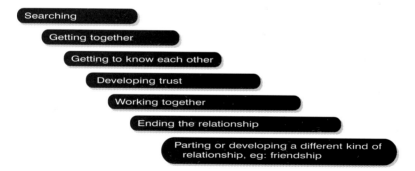

Searching

Getting together

Getting to know each other

Developing trust

Working together

Ending the relationship

Parting or developing a different kind of relationship, eg: friendship

MAINTAINING THE PARTNERSHIP

MENTOR'S ROLE

To keep the partnership going through the life cycle it is important to consider your attitude as a mentor and the climate you help to create with your mentee.

The climate needs to be relaxed, open and encouraging. This can be influenced by a number of things:

- The relationship you have previously established:
    - How well do you know the person?
    - How much trust is there already?
    - What do you have in common?
    - What are your differences?

- The level of priority you give to mentoring:
    - Is it important to you?
    - Are you aware of how beneficial mentoring can be to you, the mentee and your organisation?
    - How serious are you about the business of helping others?

MAINTAINING THE PARTNERSHIP

MENTOR'S ROLE (Cont'd)

The climate can also be helped by:

- Sitting in a relaxed manner in comfortable surroundings
- Privacy
- Asking open questions and listening carefully to the responses
- You being prepared to 'open up' about yourself
- Reviewing the ground rules and the nature of the relationship
- Having a cup of tea!

MAINTAINING THE PARTNERSHIP
MENTEE'S ROLE

As a **mentee** your attitude towards your mentor will contribute to the climate.
Be prepared to:

- Talk about yourself
- Listen and ask questions
- View this first meeting as a social event aimed at building a longer-term
  learning relationship

FROM THE FRONT LINE

> *"I very quickly realised that this particular mentor was not for me. So we discussed it and agreed to end it. There was no loss of face on anyone's part. We tried, and it didn't work out. That's fine. Think what it would have been like if we had carried on regardless!"*
>
> A mentee

HOW TO END IT

This is the only certain event in the relationship! The end may happen when the mentee has reached a stage when s/he no longer feels the need for regular contact. The mentee is confident and able to move on. It is important to consider how it will end. If the relationship has been successful, there will be cause for celebration *and* a sense of loss. Attend to both.

You may agree to meet socially or less frequently or simply call a halt.

Look back and review your mentoring relationship and what you value about it:

- What were your original goals and were they achieved?
- Did they change, did you discover new goals/aspirations?
- What problems did you have and how did you resolve them?
- Would you seek a mentoring relationship again?

FROM THE FRONT LINE

> *"When this mentoring relationship comes to an end, you will want to move on. There will be other people who come along in your life who will become your mentor."*

A mentee in financial services

TIPS FOR MENTORS & MENTEES

TIPS FOR MENTORS

1. Maintain regular contact.
2. Always be honest.
3. Avoid being judgemental.
4. Recognise that you have your own need for support. A mentor may need a mentor as well!
5. Don't expect to have all the answers.
6. Help your mentee access resources and further support.
7. Be clear about expectations and boundaries.
8. Stand back from the issues your mentee raises but work together on them.
9. Respect confidentiality.
10. If the relationship falters - hang on in there!

TIPS FOR MENTEES

1. Accept challenge willingly.
2. Share with your mentor how you feel about the way the relationship is working.
3. Maintain a positive view of yourself.
4. Be active in your own development.
5. Have faith and trust in your mentor.
6. Be willing to discuss issues openly.
7. Take a few risks in order to progress.
8. Think about other ways to develop yourself outside of your mentoring relationship.
9. Don't expect too much of your mentor.
10. Talk about the end of your relationship when the time comes.

FROM THE FRONT LINE

> *"It was my mentor who convinced me that I was good enough, so that I could convince the senior managers of my readiness for promotion."*
>
> A mentee

ISSUES & QUESTIONS

MENTOR PROFILE

Who should be a mentor?

Anyone who is interested. It may be a manager or a peer. A mentor needs to be somebody that a mentee can trust. A mentor is often, but not always, older than the mentee. A mentor may also have experience greater than, or different from, the mentee's. A mentor is someone who recognises their own need for help and support.

What about potential conflict between the line manager and the mentor?

Ideally, your mentor should not be your line manager. There is some scope for confusion of roles. Many managers see that their role includes mentoring. However, most mentees value a degree of separation between the roles.

MATCHING MENTOR TO MENTEE

How do you match people?

Often two people will match themselves without any extra help. The mentoring relationship starts from knowing each other already.

Some organisations publish lists of 'approved' mentors who are often volunteers with some training and who may provide a short pen-picture of themselves to help mentees make their choice.

Other organisations simply put people together. In this case there ought to be a logical system, clearly understood by both parties. Such a system may have as its basis common knowledge, experience and interests.

The 'dating agency' approach, using standard tests and assessments to match people, is another alternative approach.

Matching should be done sensitively and with care. Mentoring is like any other human relationship - it needs time to develop.

If you feel you would like a mentor in order to help with your development, there may be somebody you know who could fulfil the role for you. Ask them! Also, ask your Personnel/HR Department about mentoring.

ISSUES & QUESTIONS

MENTORING IN PRACTICE

How much time is involved?

This will vary depending on the mentee's needs. Average time in many organisations is 2-3 hours per month.

What about bad mentoring?

The quality of mentoring depends in part upon circumstances and the environment.
If the relationship does not work, be honest about it and either bring it to a close or try to resolve the differences.

How many mentors/mentees can I have?

It is possible to have more than one mentor. Each mentor offers something different to the mentee, most often in areas of knowledge and technical expertise. Mentors may have more than one mentee.

MENTORING IN PRACTICE

Who gets credit for mentoring?

Credit is perhaps the wrong word. Mentoring is a satisfying and productive activity for the participants and the organisation. Some organisations suggest that mentoring becomes part of an individual's Personal Development Plan.

What is the scope of mentoring?

The scope is as broad as one would want it to be. Mentoring is primarily about learning and development. Mentoring is present when there are changes and transitions to go through at work and in individual lives. A mentor recognises the links between the personal and the professional aspects of a person's life and, through the mentoring process, can help to reconcile the two.

What about confidentiality?

Confidentiality is crucial. Secrecy is inappropriate. Everything in the mentoring relationship should be done by agreement.

IMPROVING YOUR MENTORING SKILLS

Do I need training?

It is a good idea for both mentors and mentees to consider doing some training in mentoring. This will help you to:

- Understand what is involved
- Understand how to get started
- Improve your confidence and commitment to mentoring
- Improve your mentoring skills
- Seek a mentor for yourself

How do I improve as a mentor?

One way is to find a mentor for yourself. Another is to form a mentor support network with other mentors in your organisation. Further training and additional background reading (see page 86) are other options.

MENTORING IN CONTEXT

Should mentor and mentee be from the same ethnic/gender backgrounds?

In some situations this is very important. In general, the key to success is having a mentor who is able to listen, can be empathic towards the mentee and is committed to the mentee's welfare and the mentoring relationship.

Can mentoring solve all problems in the work place?

No! Mentoring is helpful in times of change, when someone starts a job or new project. Mentoring complements other development and training activities.

FURTHER READING

'Everyone needs a mentor' by David Clutterbuck, IPD
'Mentoring in action' by David Megginson & David Clutterbuck, Kogan Page
'The mentor connection' by Michael Zey, New Brunswick (USA)
'Mentoring' by Gordon F Shea, Kogan Page

Sources of information

The European Mentoring Centre is a not-for-profit organisation which maintains a library and database on mentoring, organises the annual European Mentoring Conference, and promotes research into mentoring. Membership costs £85.00 a year.

The EMC can be contacted via AMED, on 0171 235 3505 or fax 0171 235 3565.
Their website is www.mentoringcentre.org

Another useful website is the Mentors Forum, which you can find on
www.mentorsforum.co.uk

About the authors

This book was produced collaboratively by the following people, all of whom are lecturers at the University of Durham.

Geof Alred, MA, Ph.D, Dip.Counselling, BAC AccT.
Geof has wide experience of education, training and professional development. He is a counsellor and counsellor trainer. His consultancy and research interests include mentoring and learning in organisations.

Bob Garvey, Cert.Ed., MA.
Bob works with individuals and organisations helping them to understand and apply mentoring in the work place. He has published extensively on the subject of mentoring in both academic and professional journals. Bob is both a mentor and a mentee.

Richard Smith, BA, M.Ed.
Richard has wide experience of training, mentoring and promoting 'learning organisations', both in the UK and beyond. He has a particular interest in ethical issues, as well as in education in all its dimensions.

ORDER FORM

Your details

Name _____

Position _____

Company _____

Address _____

_____

_____

Telephone _____

Facsimile _____

E-mail _____

VAT No. (EC companies) _____

Your Order Ref _____

Please send me:

No. copies

The Mentoring _____ Pocketbook ☐

The _____ Pocketbook ☐

The _____ Pocketbook ☐

The _____ Pocketbook ☐

The _____ Pocketbook ☐

Order by Post

MANAGEMENT POCKETBOOKS LTD

14 EAST STREET ALRESFORD HAMPSHIRE SO24 9EE UK

Order by Phone, Fax or Internet

Telephone: +44 (0)1962 735573
Facsimile: +44 (0)1962 733637
E-mail: pocketbks@aol.com
http://members.aol.com/pocketbks

Customers in USA should contact:
Stylus Publishing, LLC, 22883 Quicksilver Drive,
Sterling, VA 20166-2012 Telephone: 703 661 1500
Facsimile: 703 661 1501 E-mail: styluspub@aol.com

THE MANAGEMENT POCKETBOOK SERIES

Pocketbooks

Appraisals Pocketbook
Assertiveness Pocketbook
Balance Sheet Pocketbook
Business Planning Pocketbook
Business Presenter's Pocketbook
Business Writing Pocketbook
Challengers Pocketbook
Coaching Pocketbook
Communicator's Pocketbook
Creative Manager's Pocketbook
Cultural Gaffes Pocketbook
Customer Service Pocketbook
Empowerment Pocketbook
Export Pocketbook
Facilitator's Pocketbook
Improving Profitability Pocketbook
Interviewer's Pocketbook
Key Account Manager's Pocketbook
Learner's Pocketbook

Managing Budgets Pocketbook
Managing Cashflow Pocketbook
Managing Change Pocketbook
Managing Your Appraisal Pocketbook
Manager's Pocketbook
Manager's Training Pocketbook
Marketing Pocketbook
Meetings Pocketbook
Mentoring Pocketbook
Motivation Pocketbook
Negotiator's Pocketbook
People Manager's Pocketbook
Performance Management Pocketbook
Project Management Pocketbook
Quality Pocketbook
Sales Excellence Pocketbook
Salesperson's Pocketbook
Self-managed Development Pocketbook
Stress Pocketbook
Teamworking Pocketbook

Telephone Skills Pocketbook
Telesales Pocketbook
Thinker's Pocketbook
Time Management Pocketbook
Trainer Standards Pocketbook
Trainer's Pocketbook

Pocketfiles/Other

Leadership: Sharing The Passion
The Great Presentation Scandal
Trainer's Blue Pocketfile of
Ready-to-use Exercises
Trainer's Green Pocketfile of
Ready-to-use Exercises
Trainer's Red Pocketfile of
Ready-to-use Exercises

Audio Cassettes

Tips for Presenters
Tips for Trainers